A barrister with nearly 30 years in practice, both as a self-employed barrister and whilst employed by the Crown Prosecution Service. Andrea Pitt is also a fee paid Employment Judge and a Legally Qualified Chair for Police Misconduct Hearings.

After her border terrier, Jasper, came into her life she discovered that dog ownership was an area of law where people were unsure of their responsibilities and their rights, and that the only books available were designed for professionals. She has since written articles for 'Lines' the Northern Border Terrier annual book, and is putting together seminars aimed at the general public. The first one at 'Borderfest', a gathering for Border terrier owners was well received.

Andrea has a general interest in animal welfare, in particular dogs, and is a member of the Association of Lawyers for Animal Welfare.

A Practical Guide to Dog Law for Owners and Others

A Practical Guide to Dog Law for Owners and Others

Andrea E Pitt
Barrister at Law
Sole Practitioner
LLB Hons
Employment Judge (Fee Paid)
Crime, Employment, Dog Law

Law Brief Publishing

© Andrea Pitt

All rights reserved. No part of this publication may be reproduced, stored in a retrieval system, or transmitted, in any form or by any means, electronic, mechanical, photocopying, recording or otherwise, without the prior permission of the publisher.

Excerpts from judgments and statutes are Crown copyright. Any Crown Copyright material is reproduced with the permission of the Controller of OPSI and the Queen's Printer for Scotland. Some quotations may be licensed under the terms of the Open Government Licence (http://www.nationalarchives.gov.uk/doc/open-government-licence/version/3).

Cover image © iStockphoto.com/Pekic

The information in this book was believed to be correct at the time of writing. All content is for information purposes only and is not intended as legal advice. No liability is accepted by either the publisher or author for any errors or omissions (whether negligent or not) that it may contain. Professional advice should always be obtained before applying any information to particular circumstances.

Published 2017 by
Law Brief Publishing
30 The Parks
Minehead
Somerset
TA24 8BT

www.lawbriefpublishing.com

Paperback: 978-1-911035-26-8

To John and Esme,
who gave me a love
for border terriers and
so much more

PREFACE

My border terrier, Jasper, came into my life 6 years ago. At that time I knew very little about dogs, their behaviour or the law relating to them; I had to learn fast!

A chance conversation with a member of the Northern Border Terrier Club led me to believe that this was an area of law where people were unsure of their responsibilities and their rights. As a result I started 'boning' up in this area and realised that the only books available were designed for professionals. I wrote a short article for the Northern Border Terrier annual book and my second is in this year's edition.

This book is aimed at the general dog owner who has no knowledge of the law but wishes to ensure they are aware of their rights and responsibilities and to try to ensure they do not fall foul of the law. In addition to make them aware of their rights if something goes wrong. I have pulled together information from a number of sources such as the general UK law and guidance issued from organisations such as DEFRA so you don't have to go digging around for it.

The guide begins with the acquiring of a puppy in the process when you acquire your dog and works though your dog's life until the end of your time together.

I have pulled together the areas where the law impacts upon you as a dog owner, breeder, walker, groomer or victim. It is not intended to be a comprehensive statement, but a guide to everything to do with dogs, covering frequent areas of concern. If you have an issue there is no substitute for proper legal advice… but I would say that!

I am a proponent of educating people to hopefully ensure you know what you can and cannot do. This book is not designed to worry you or put you off owning a dog, which can bring substantial rewards, but rather to guide you away from pitfalls and to assist when things do go wrong.

Good Luck and enjoy your dog safely.

Andrea and Jasper the Border Terrier
July 2017

Contents

Chapter One	The First Step: Buying and Selling	1
Chapter Two	The Basics of Ownership: Or How Your Life Will Change	7
Chapter Three	Dangerous Dogs	17
Chapter Four	Other Criminal Offences: It's Not Just Dangerous Dogs	33
Chapter Five	Irresponsible Dog Owners: Other Ways the Law Gets Involved	41
Chapter Six	The Dog in Your Home: Even Here the Law May Get You	49
Chapter Seven	The Dog Outside Your Home: The Perils of Outside	55
Chapter Eight	Travelling With Your Dog: Buses, Planes, Trains and Automobiles	63
Chapter Nine	Animal Welfare: Looking After Your Dog	69
Chapter Ten	End of Life: Time to Say Goodbye	83
Chapter Eleven	Legal Procedures: If It All Goes Wrong	87
Important Information and Aide-Memoire		97

CHAPTER ONE
THE FIRST STEP:
BUYING AND SELLING

In this Chapter I look at the ways in which dogs come into our lives, including contracts for buying and selling puppies and dogs, and other ways you may acquire a puppy such as rehoming.

Buying a Dog

Many people buy a puppy from a breeder, but there are still so called 'puppy farms' out there. You must remember that a dog is a 'chattel' (more later) in the eyes of the law and, other than basic welfare issues, an animal can be bought and sold in the same way as a car. When an item is bought the buyer and seller form a contract in the same way which will contain terms and conditions. Of course, when buying your dog or puppy, the last thing on your mind is contract law but here are some hints and tips.

General

A contract does not have to be written down – it can be oral; that is to say the issues you discuss with the breeder. If the contract is written down it will contain the main terms, for example; John Smith is selling a border terrier to Ann White for £500. It will usually be an implied term of the sale that the dog is 'fit for purpose'. This means that the dog is fit and healthy and, as far as can be ascertained, free from disease or injury. It does not necessarily mean that if you buy a breed of dog which is prone to a particular type of disease or physical impairment which arises after purchase that you will have a remedy; the answer is to do your homework.

Breeders

It is always best when selling anything to have it in writing. This is especially so if you want to have any specific terms of sale for the buyer to agree to.

You may ask a prospective buyer to agree to any terms you wish, as long as it is legal. For example you may wish to prohibit the dog being shown, either a total prohibition or in any show which may allow the dog to obtain a Challenge Certificate.

The main term you may wish to look at is a prohibition on breeding – either a total prohibition or breeding without your permission. This may be important to you (and the owner of the Sire) to protect your breeding lines.

Of course it is up to you whether to sell to any particular person.

Buyers

The information for breeders is also relevant but remember the most important thing to do is to ask questions – how big will it get; how much will I spend on food; how much exercise?

In particular, before you agree to buy ask about the parents and grandparents health; are any of them suffering from the diseases common to your breed. If you are not happy, don't buy. After you have bought it is too late to change your mind.

Endorsements

The Kennel Club has the option where the dog to be sold can have an endorsement upon its registration. Regulation B12 of the Kennel Club Regulations permits two types of registration – first 'Progeny not eligible for registration'; secondly 'Not eligible of issue of an export pedigree'.

In order to place either endorsement on a dogs record you must have physical possession of the dog at the time the endorsement is sought.

You MUST bring the endorsement to the attention of the buyer and this must be evidenced in writing at the time of the sale; if you fail to do this and there is a dispute, the Kennel Club will rule in favour of the new owner. For full information on this topic check out the full text on the Kennel Club website.

Kennels

Kennels is not a technical term under the law; the phrase used is 'Breeding Establishment' which is technically based on the number of litters a bitch has in any one year.

If it falls within this definition it will be subject certain rules.

Kennels or Breeding Establishments are dealt with in more detail under 'Welfare'.

Rehoming Centres

Rehoming centres will often require your dog to be neutered and require a fee to be paid.

An issue that may concern you is if the dog was a stray, what happens if the original owner turns up?

In such a case you will have a measure of protection under the Environmental Protection Act section 149 (7).

Where a stray is recovered by the Local Authority and then rehomed after 7 days the person who is rehoming acquires the rights of the owner as long as this is done in good faith.

Other Rehomings

If you are taking over a dog from anyone else, always check they can give up possession to you, i.e. that the dog is theirs. If you are satisfied they are able to lawfully sell the dog I would advise that you put the transaction down in writing which is signed by both parties and dated, The document should make it clear that the other party are relinquisihing all rights in the dog. In the event that there is dispute later it may an Important document to show that you obtained the dog in good faith or that the seller gave the dog up to you.

Children

Under Secton 3 Pet Animals Act It is illegal to sell an animal as a pet to someone you reasonably believe to be under 12 years of age. This means that if a family arrive to buy a pup for their 7 year old you must actually sell it to the parent(s). It matters not if you are a private breeder or a pet shop.

The Sale of Goods Act 1979

As a chattel, this Act does impact on the sale of dogs. For example it will be a term of a contract for sale that the seller is entiled to sell the dog. Further, that the dog is fit for the purpose it is sold. That is to say – if the seller is aware that the dog is bought for a particular purpose it is reasonably fit to carry it out. For example, knowing someone wanted to breed from it but sold a bitch knowing she may have an inherited condition which makes it inadvisable to do so.

If it goes wrong

If you believe that there is a problem and it cannot be resolved amicably with the person from whom you acquired the dog or puppy you may be able to take action through the County Court as a small claim.

The options available to you will depend upon whether the problem involves a term which is a 'condition' or a 'warranty'. A condition is a term which goes to the heart of the contract and it may entitle you to return the dog and get your money back; or you could ask for the difference in the value between the dog you have and the dog you believed you had bought.

A warranty is a lesser term; an example might be that you were told the puppy has been wormed; in this case you can claim for damages as a result of having to have the dog wormed.

Summary

Dogs come into our lives in a variety of ways, some conventional other less so; the key to getting the correct puppy for you that is fit and healthy is to do your homework before you make any decisions. If signing a contract, make sure you know what it all means.

CHAPTER TWO
THE BASICS OF OWNERSHIP: OR HOW YOUR LIFE WILL CHANGE

In this Chapter I examine the issue of ownership of a dog, your obligations under the law as to identification of yourself as the owner, and the consequences of not having an ID tag. Also, the concept of your dog being treated as a possession, in particular for the purposes of the criminal law.

The Dog as a possession

Under the law dogs, in common with all animals, are treated as a 'chattel' or a possession in the same way as your car is. It may be that you have to establish you are or are not the owner of your pet, for example if you are in dispute with a partner or are subject to criminal proceedings.

Owner / Keeper / In Charge

Under different legislation there is a variety of expressions used to describe a person who has a dog. Under the Micro-chipping of Dogs (England) Regulations 2015, and similar Regulations in Scotland Wales and Northern Ireland, the regulations apply to a keeper. Under the Dangerous Dogs Act the offences apply to the owner and/or the person in charge.

It is unlikely you have a piece of paper which explicitly states you are one of the above but some legislation has a definition and some does not.

If there is a dispute as to who is an owner, the law will look at all the circumstances to determine ownership. Factors taken into account may be: who is the declared owner on the microchip; if the dog is registered with the kennel club, who is named on the pedigree certificate; where does the dog normally live, or with whom; who pays the bills for the dog?

If you are in dispute with someone concerning ownership of a dog you are entitled to make a claim in the County Court.

In Charge

This is an important concept because in some circumstances it may absolve you of guilt in a criminal case. These are where you have entrusted the care of your dog to another person. This has to be a person you reasonably believed to be a fit and proper person to shift responsibility.

Other types of ownership

Under the Dangerous Dogs Act a person under 16 cannot be an owner for the purpose of a prosecution. So one of the questions you may want to ask yourself is "should I allow my child to walk my dog?" As it may be if something goes wrong you will be held responsible in the criminal law and may be prosecuted.

Keeper

The keeper of a dog may sometimes be the owner but may be a different person entirely, for example if a breeder retains ownership of a dog.

The law regulates the keeper of an assistance dog in three ways. You will be the keeper if you are the body responsible for training, for such period as the dog is undergoing training; after it has ceased training if you are the person with whom it normally resides; or for a new born puppy the keeper is the owner of the bitch who gave birth. For any other dog the keeper is person with whom he normally resides.

Microchipping and ID tags

As from 1st April 2016 all dogs in England, Scotland, Wales and Northern Ireland must be microchipped with a registered company within 8 weeks of birth. If you are buying from a breeder it is imperative you check whether the puppy has been chipped before you collect it. The penalty for failure is a level 4 fine in the magistrate's court.

If you buy a dog or puppy you must change the registration with the microchip company unless the seller has already done so. The regulations do not state a time within which this must be done.

The seller MUST not sell unless the dog has been microchipped

If you import a dog which is not microchipped into the country, you have 30 days to ensure it is microchipped.

There are exceptions in relation to working dogs and dogs which may have an adverse reaction.

Tattoos are commonplace today and many owners prefer them, but they DO NOT comply with the legal requirements and your dog still needs his collar. The law requires that all dogs in a public place have a collar and an ID tag. The tag MUST have the owners name and address upon it. A public place is in essence a place where the public go. It includes places such as parks where you have to pay an entry fee. If your dog for any reason is found wandering without you, the police or a dog warden has authority to seize your dog which may have serious consequences if you do not collect your dog.

Part of the reason why identification of you as the owner is so important is the responsibility of the Local Council if your dog strays.

The council is obliged to keep list of all dogs recovered. Under the Environmental Protection Act the Local Authority have the power to dispose of your dog if it is not claimed within seven days, or seven days of a notice being served upon the owner. If this happens and the dog is rehomed, in good faith, you will lose your legal right to your dog. Currently there is no obligation for any person, be it a Local Authority, rehoming centre or vet, to check for a microchip so the ID tag is the best way for them to discover the owner. It may that if your dog is rehomed under the section AND is microchipped AND up to date that you could argue that the good faith part is not made out and you can seek return of the dog.

If you do lose your dog and recover it you may be charged the costs of kennelling

Insurance

"Do I need insurance?" is a question I am frequently asked. My advice is always "yes". Pet insurance doesn't just cover vet bills, it can cover other areas too. Although pet insurance is sold on the basis that it pays for your vet's fees it usually does more than that.

The right policy will cover you in relation to claims made by other people, for example if your dog knocks someone over in the street. This is called third party liability. It may also assist with your legal costs in such a claim.

It is always worthwhile checking your household insurance policy as well, as this may give you some cover.

The Criminal Law

Dog Fouling

This is a huge issue which makes the general public very anti-dog. Apart from the smell there is a risk of contracting toxo-cairiasis. This is caused by a parasite found in dog, cat and fox faeces. Children are particularly susceptible to contracting it because of their tendency to play and to place contaminated items, such as hands which have been near faeces, into their mouths. Whilst the basic infection may be treated, there is a risk of damage to the eyes and possible blindness as a result. It is for this reason that dog fouling is treated so seriously.

Dogs (Fouling of Land) Act 1996 makes it an offence not to remove dog faeces from designated land. The basic rule is that the land is open to the air and the public are permitted to use it. There are some exceptions but it is perhaps best just to remember to pick it up and bin it. It will not be a defence if you did not know about the faeces or that you did not have anything to put it in.

It may also come under a Public Spaces Protection Order (see later under 'irresponsible dog owners').

Dogs as possessions

As we have already seen, a dog is a possession and as such can be treated as stolen property and should be reported to the police if that is case. Additionally, if someone harms your animal, for example by kicking it, this may amount to an offence of criminal damage and may also be reported to the police. The following offences may be committed.

Theft

Theft is the defined as dishonest appropriation of property (your dog) belonging to another with the intention to permanently deprive. What a mouthful! If someone takes your dog they will be guilty if they intended to keep it or in some other way treat it as if they were the owner, for example by selling it. They have to be dishonest in doing this, which is assessed by the standards of the ordinary man in the street, would their actions be considered to be dishonest? It is not what they, the person who took the dog think.

Dogs owned by more than one person. This is a tricky area especially where a relationship breaks down and one person asserts a right to a dog. It is unlikely in this situation that the police will get involved and consider it to be more of a civil dispute as a person cannot steal their own property. Even if you are of the view, and can prove it, it is unlikely the police will act.

As a chattel, if your dog is stolen from inside your house or another building this will be burglary. In particular, if this is an invasion of your home the law treats such an offence very seriously.

A note of caution about the use of Facebook. Whilst it is an extremely useful tool in seeking the return of animals whether lost or stolen, beware that if you offer a reward with no questions asked you may be committing a criminal offence for which you may be fined.

I always advise people to err on the side of caution before posting any videos or pictures on Facebook as they may compromise an investigation. If your animal is stolen and you have such evidence, hand it over to the police and ask their advice before doing anything else.

In particular, be careful in the language you use; although you may think that the people are scumbags you could land yourself in trouble for such language.

There are pressure groups trying to make change in the law to ensure that where a dog is stolen, it is not treated the same as a car.

Criminal Damage

Again, as a chattel your dog can be damaged. Although this may be a cruelty issue the offence of criminal damage is a useful tool if any other offence is difficult to prove, In addition, it may that someone will accept causing damage to an animal rather than cruelty.

Criminal damage is the intentional or reckless causing of damage to your dog without lawful excuse. For example, if someone deliberately kicks your dog, without any reason and injures it, this will be criminal damage.

The difficulties come in situations where a person alleges they had a reasonable excuse for their actions. The phrase 'lawful excuse' is only partially defined but does include protection of property and other general defences. This extends the definition to include self-defence of you or another person.

The latter would apply for example, where your child is under attack from a dog and you kick out to protect your child. However, this does not give you an absolute right to injure the dog; in defending yourself or your child you are only permitted to do that which is reasonably necessary. If you kick out several times but the dog retreated after one blow you may be guilty of an offence.

Dogs in hot cars

This regularly crops up when the UK has those rare summer days. Can you smash a car window to rescue a dog? The simple answer is 'yes', if it is necessary to protect the animal from suffering. But there are a number of factors to consider before you do so – How hot is it? How long has the owner been absent? How distressed is the dog? What attempts have been made to contact the owner or the police? It will be difficult to judge these to a nicety, however where it is absolutely necessary to get to the animal it is probable that you will have a defence. With the availability of cameras on phones and apps for temperatures it will always be best to document what you are doing.

Finally, it is still a requirement under The Road Traffic Act to report an accident involving a dog to the police.

Summary

To be the owner of a dog carries with it a number of responsibilities and challenges a few of which were touched on here. You may avoid liability if you have asked someone else to be in charge of your dog. As a possession the criminal law makes it an offence to steal your dog.

CHAPTER THREE
DANGEROUS DOGS

In this Chapter I look at the area which brings most concern for owners – dogs which are dangerous. I will look at the definitions and penalties for criminal offences and a civil complaint. I will also look at Breed specific legislation.

If your dog is involved in an incident the police may become involved and you may end up in court in a number of ways. The most common are:

A <u>complaint</u> may be made that your dog was dangerous and not under proper control – Dogs Act 1871.

A criminal charge for being the owner or in charge of a dog dangerously out of control – Dangerous Dogs Act 1991.

It is important to understand the differences between the two; not only are the penalties vastly different but also the way they are prosecuted and this is dealt with in the chapter eleven, 'Legal Procedures'.

<u>Dogs Act 1871</u>

This Act gives a Magistrates Court the ability to make an order that a dog be kept under proper control or be destroyed. In order to do so the court must be satisfied that the dog is dangerous AND not kept under proper control.

Whether a dog is under proper control is a question of fact not law although there is some guidance in the case law, for example if your dog is not on a lead it may be said to not to be under proper control. In relation to dangerousness, unlike the DDA (Dangerous Dogs Act), no injury has to be proved, or it can be an injury to another dog. It is for this reason that it is frequently used. Be aware that if your dog chases sheep or injures cattle it will be considered to be dangerous. You should also be aware that the fact that you did not know your dog was dangerous is not a defence, nor is the 'but it's never happened before' observation although it may be mitigation.

Many owners are concerned by the phrase 'or destroyed'. It is usual, save in exceptional cases, after a first incident, for an order to keep the dog under proper control. This may include conditions which are wide ranging but may include neutering if male, muzzling, keeping on a lead and prohibition from certain places, such as public parks.

In addition you may be disqualified from having custody of a dog for a period of time. Note this doesn't prevent ownership but that for the period of disqualification the dog must live with and be walked by someone else.

It is a criminal offence to breach any orders made. If found guilty you could be fined and if not previously ordered, disqualified from having custody of a dog.

Penalty

There is no financial penalty as such, although you may be asked to pay costs associated with bringing the case to court. The penalty is the risk to your dog, which is discussed later.

Dangerous Dogs Act 1991

This is the act you are probably more aware of and if you fall foul of any of its provisions there are serious consequences for you and your dog.

The Act was introduced 'to prohibit persons from having in their possession or custody dogs belonging to types bred for fighting; to impose restrictions in respect of such dogs pending the coming into force of the prohibition; to enable restrictions to be imposed in relation to other types of dog which present a serious danger to the public; to make further provision for securing that dogs are kept under proper control; and for connected purposes'. It arose out of concerns in relation to dog attacks particularly on children and to fill in the gaps in the Dogs Act 1871

Banned Breeds

The most controversial part of the act is section 1, relating to 'banned' breeds. There is often confusion about which dogs it applies to. It is headed 'Dogs bred for fighting' which gives an indication of those it is directed at. It specifies any dog of the type known as pit bull; any dog of the type known as a

Japanese Tosa and any dog 'being a type appearing …to be bred for fighting OR to have the characteristics of a TYPE bred for that purpose'. Dogo Argentino and Fila Brazilero have been added as banned breeds by the Secretary of State under this part of the Act.

This is where the confusion lies, your dog does not have to be a pit bull or one of the other types to fall foul of the section, but simply to have the characteristics of a pit bull. How is this established? Your dog will be examined by an expert, usually the Dog Legislation Officer – a police officer who has experience and training in all areas of dog law. He will assess your dog in accordance with the American Dog Breeders Association standard of conformation. In order to be a 'type' your dog must have a substantial number of characteristics which makes it more pit bull terrier than any other type.

If your dog is considered to be a pit bull type it may be seized by the police or local authority until its breed or type is established. This can be done by agreement or via the courts. If you wish to challenge the authorities you will invariably need evidence from a suitable expert. The presumption is that the dog is the breed/type alleged unless you can establish it is not.

However, if you have any of the dogs listed you MUST not breed; sell or exchange; advertise for sale or exchange; or abandon. In a public place the dog MUST wear a muzzle to prevent biting and must be on a lead held by a person over 16 years of age.

When the act first became law it was possible to have dogs exempted, rather than destroyed. The exemption applies only to dogs born before the act came into force. This makes sense as since that date it is an offence to breed such dogs.

However IF your dog is seized and you are prosecuted for one of the offences it is possible for the court to order your dog to be placed on the Exemption Register. You cannot apply (as you might for a driving licence) to exempt your dog.

An exemption, if granted, is subject to conditions. The dog must be neutered, whether male or female. This must be carried out by a vet who shall provide the dog with a permanent identification to the effect the operation has been carried out. You must have third party liability insurance.

Once you have an exemption certificate there are ongoing requirements as to notification of ownership and address, muzzling and keeping on a lead. The dog must be kept securely to ensure it cannot escape and it must be tattooed and microchipped.

Even if you comply with all the requirements, remember you are still subject to the laws concerning dangerous dogs.

The maximum penalty for you is 6 months imprisonment and or a level 5 fine (unlimited amount since March 2015).

Dogs not under proper control

This is the section that most people are aware of and it is the one you are most likely to fall foul of.

Section 3 places a duty on an owner or a person in charge to ensure that their dog is kept under control in a public place. It is set out below:

(1) If a dog is dangerously out of control in any place in England or Wales–

(a) The owner; and

(b) If different, the person for the time being in charge of the dog,

Is guilty of an offence, or, if the dog while so out of control injures any person, an aggravated offence, under this subsection.

(2) In proceedings for an offence under subsection (1) above against a person who is the owner of a dog but was not at the material time in charge of it, it shall be a defense for the accused to prove that the dog was at the material time in the charge of a person whom he reasonably believed to be a fit and proper person to be in charge of it.

(3) If the owner or, if different, the person for the time being in charge of a dog allows it to enter a place which is not a public place but where it is not permitted to be and while it is there–

(a) It injures any person or an assistance dog; or

(b) There are grounds for reasonable apprehension that it will do so,

He is guilty of an offence, or, if the dog injures any person, an aggravated offence, under this subsection.

This makes it a criminal offence to own a 'dangerous dog'.

What is a dangerous dog? The act makes it clear that your dog is dangerous if:

> *'On any occasion on which there are grounds for reasonable apprehension that it will injure any person, whether or not it actually does so'.*

This is quite a wide definition and deliberately so. It means that all cases will turn upon their own unique facts. The first point to note is that the dog does not have to actually cause an injury, there simply has to be an apprehension (fear) that it will. That fear must be reasonable, that is to say if viewed by another person it was likely to happen. So it is clear that a dog on dog attack MAY fulfil the criteria to be a dangerous dog if someone fears that they, themselves, may be injured.

What does that mean? The comments in relation to the Dogs Act, above, are relevant. I always advise people that if they cannot bring their dog immediately to heel they do not have control of it, however this of itself does not make it dangerous.

Shortly after the act was introduced the concept was examined by the courts on a specific point of law called 'strict liability. The facts of the cases are useful examples of what may be considered dangerous.

Mr Bezzina was exercising his Rottweiler dog, at the time, off its lead, in a small grassy compound. Some teenagers were nearby. There was some sort of confrontation between them

Mr Bezzina. At some stage during that confrontation Mr Bezzina's dog suddenly chased after one of those teenagers and bit his back, causing injury, and continued to chase the teenager until he managed to escape into a nearby police station.

In the next example there appeared no reason for the incident. The dog owner, Ms Codling, was walking her dog off lead. A Mr Green was also walking his dog. It seems there was an incident involving the dogs during which Mr Green was bitten. There was no explanation as to why Ms Codling's dog had bitten him.

The final example relates to a Mr Elvin. It appears he was the owner of two powerful and dangerous pit bull dogs, which the Judge considered to have been left in 'inadequately secured' premises, who got out and bit a male who was nearby. The important point here is that Mr Elvin believed he had secured the dogs, but this was not a valid defence.

What we learn from these three cases is that once the facts of the case have been established – that the dog is in a public place; that the owner has been correctly identified and that the dog was dangerously out of control – it matters not if you, the owner or person in charge, were not aware the dog would act in this way. The Judge, Lord Justice Kennedy, said that the onus is on the owner to ensure that he takes effective steps to ensure that it does not happen, for example keeping the dog on a lead or ensuring the premises are sufficiently secure to keep the dog inside.

In the criminal law this is called strict liability; it means that it doesn't matter what your intention was. If the facts are proved then you are guilty.

He gave an example. If a child pokes a stick at your dog and it reacts he suggested you would be guilty.

The law however is never static and has now moved on due on to a case involving Mr Robinson-Pierre. The facts are that RP was at home and his dog, a pit bull was secure inside the property. The police attended and lawfully entered the house using an enforcer. The dog which was upstairs came down and immediately attacked that officer who was backing away. The dog went on to attack other officers, outside of the house, who went to the aid of the first. When RP appeared and was asked to call the dog off he told officers there was nothing he could do. In all, five officers were injured. When he was arrested RP said 'it wasn't the dog's fault you should have knocked'. The first incident inside the house was dismissed because it occurred inside private property. (This was 2013 before the law changed as you will see later). RP argued he shouldn't be responsible for the actions of the dog because he had done nothing to allow the dog to escape OR cause it to be dangerously out of control. He was convicted and appealed because under Bezzina, although the owner had done nothing wrong, the dog was dangerously out of control.

The Court of Appeal re-examined the Bezzina case (and the others) and concluded that there may be circumstances where the rule didn't apply. The court said that an owner will only be guilty if they by 'act or omission had made more than a minimal contribution to the prohibited state of affairs'. If the owner did nothing to bring about the state of affairs or by inaction allowed the state of affairs to arise. RPs conviction was overturned, however it is possible that he would still be guilty because he did nothing to get the dog off the officers after he became aware of the situation.

Looking at all this in layman's terms; if your dog for no reason attacks another dog or a person, your dog will undoubtedly be 'dangerously out of control'. If we take the example of the child poking a stick at a dog; you may still be guilty if you did nothing to stop it by telling the child not to do that. However it is unlikely you will be guilty if, as in Mr Elvin's case, the dogs had been adequately secured on the property.

If you do find yourself before the court the CPS will have to prove not only that you were the owner of the dog involved, but also that the dog is correctly identified as the one responsible. For example if there are two black Labradors on a field and one bites a person the CPS have to prove it was YOUR black lab.

The penalty for you is different depending on which court hears your case and how serious it is. In the Magistrates Court you can be imprisoned for 6 months and/or fined at Level 5.

If the case is dealt with at the Crown Court and the case is where a person has died as a result of the injury you may be sent to prison for 14 years and be fined. If a person was injured as a result of the dog you may be sent to prison for 5 years.

Finally, as already noted, if the dog is owned by someone under 16 years of age the act makes the 'head of the household' responsible. This means that if your 15 year old son owns a dog and walks it and there is an incident you could find yourself in court!

Defences

It is a defence if, as an owner, you were not in charge of the dog at the time of the incident but had left it with a person you reasonably believed was a fit and proper person so that you are not responsible. This could be a professional dog walker or your partner. A word of caution however – if you allow your 10 year old daughter to walk your dog, even a very small breed, on her own and there is an incident it is likely that this defence will not apply.

The Householder defence

It has been well publicised that the Dangerous Dogs Act had a major flaw when it was first introduced, as can be seen from RP. It only applied in public places which meant many of those horrific cases involving young children did not fall within the ambit of the law. The Act was changed to take out the words 'public place' and make it any place in England and Wales. This extension meant that an offence could be committed inside a property.

Having looked at the cases above it is clear that this might leave people open to prosecution in circumstances where it may be considered morally wrong. The law therefore provides for what is called the householder defence. The section provides

> *(1A) A person (D) is not guilty of an offence under subsection (1) in a case which is a householder case*
>
> *(1B) For the purposes of subsection 1A " a householder case" is a case where*
>
> *(a) The dog is dangerously out of control while in or partly in a building , or part of a building ,that is a dwelling or is forces accommodation (or is both), and*
>
> *(b) At that time*
>
> *(i) The person to who the dog is dangerously out of control (V) is in or entering the building or part as a trespasser, or*
>
> *(ii) D if present at the time believed V to be in, or entering, the building or part as a trespasser.*

The defence only applies to a dwelling that is a place somewhere where people live. It will not apply to other places such as a warehouse and it does not apply to any land around your home, such as your garden or a paddock.

It only gives you a partial defence towards people who are trespassers or you believe to be trespassers. Two issues arise here – who is a trespasser, and what is meant by 'believe'?

A trespasser is defined as a person who enters your property without your consent, whether this is a deliberate entry or they were negligent in entering your property or reckless in entering. If we go back to the situation in RP; the officers would not be trespassers because they had a warrant to enter. If they didn't have a warrant then the defence would apply. Although simply stated 'believed' seems easy to understand, however it will be for you to establish that you did believe the person was a trespasser and this will depend on the facts of each case.

Assistance Dogs

After some attacks on assistance dogs there is, now, a specific offence in relation to assistance dogs. There is no definition of assistance dogs but it is likely to cover guide dogs, hearing dogs etc.

Control Orders and Destruction

Under both the Dogs Act and the Dangerous Dogs Act the court has power to make the following orders – a control order, a destruction order, or a contingent destruction order. Section 4 gives the court the power to destroy, and when it first came into force it was mandatory for an offence under section 1 or an aggravated offence under section 3. However the law has been relaxed by the insertion of the subsection 4(1A):

> *'Nothing shall require the court to order the destruction of a dog if the court is satisfied*

(a) That the dog would not constitute a danger to public safety

(b) [Where the dog is prohibited] there is a good reason why the dog has not been exempted.

Where the court was previously required to make a destruction order it may now make a Contingent Destruction Order; that is an order that the owner keeps the dog under proper control or it will be destroyed. The courts may, and usually do, impose conditions on how this is to be achieved. These may include neutering, muzzling and keeping on a lead. This is not an exhaustive list and may include ensuring a dog is kept securely to prevent escape.

It addition, a court may order a dog destroyed where a dog has been seized, even if the owner is not convicted, because they cannot be found, or for any other reason or because the dog is a prohibited breed. Again the court does not have to order destruction if it is satisfied that the dog would not constitute a danger to public safety.

The issue of destruction was considered by the Court of Appeal in Flack. The following guidance was given on how a court should approach an application for destruction:

(1) The court is empowered under section 4(1) of the 1991 Act to order the destruction of the dog.

(2) Nothing in that provision shall require the court to order destruction if the court is satisfied that the dog

would not constitute a danger to public safety: section 4(1)(a) of the 1991 Act.

(3) The court should ordinarily consider, before ordering immediate destruction, whether to exercise the power under section 4a (4) of the 1991 Act to order that, unless the owner of the dog keeps it under proper control, the dog shall be destroyed ("a suspended order of destruction").

(4) A suspended order of destruction under that provision may specify the measures to be taken by the owner for keeping the dog under control whether by muzzling, keeping it on a lead, or excluding it from a specified place or otherwise: see section 4(a)(5) of the 1991 Act.

(5) A court should not order destruction if satisfied that the imposition of such a condition would mean the dog would not constitute a danger to public safety.

(6) In deciding what order to make, the court must consider all the relevant circumstances which include the dog's history of aggressive behaviour and the owner's history of controlling the dog concerned in order to determine what order should be made.

This makes it clear that a court should not make an order for destruction unless a suspended (or contingent) order would ensure the safety of the general public.

Ferocious Dogs

Although seldom used these days there is an additional law you need to be aware of – the Town and Police Clauses Act. It is still on the statute books so be aware.

It is an offence to let an unmuzzled ferocious dog be at large so that it obstructs or annoys the residents or passengers in the street or puts them in danger, or to urge any dog to attack worry or put in fear any person or animal.

This act does include incidents involving other animals so it is useful to be aware of it. 'At large' is not defined but will probably mean dogs NOT on a lead. The dog doesn't have to actually cause fear or injury, but simply obstruct or annoy, which should be given their ordinary meaning.

There is no provision for the dog to be destroyed and it merely carries a fine as penalty, so is little used today.

Summary

Any dog owner can find themselves before the court if they do not have proper control of their dog whilst out in public. It can be a minor incident or much more serious, especially if it involves a child. The answer is to always be aware of where your dog is, perhaps don't use Facebook or the phone when walking, but concentrate on your dog and you should be ok.

CHAPTER FOUR
OTHER CRIMINAL OFFENCES: IT'S NOT JUST DANGEROUS DOGS

In this chapter I look at other criminal offences which may involve you and your dog which are not covered elsewhere.

<u>Hunting with Dogs</u>

The Hunting Act 2004 made it an offence to hunt a wild mammal with a dog unless the hunting is exempt. A wild mammal has a wide interpretation; it not only includes a mammal living wild, such as a badger but also a wild mammal which has been bred or tamed; which is in captivity or confinement; which has been released from or escaped from confinement.

Hunting with a dog includes a person taking part in a pursuit of a wild mammal where one or more dogs are employed in that pursuit. This applies even if the dogs are not under that person's control, e.g. they may be under the control of the hunt master.

It is also an offence to assist in hunting by knowingly permitting your land to be used in the course of the commission of an offence or to knowingly permit a dog you own to be used in hunting. This means you do not have to be present, but if you allow someone to take your dog knowing it is to be used for hunting, you will be guilty of an offence.

Hare Coursing is a specific offence. This is defined as a competition in which dogs are, by the use of live hares, assessed as to skill in hunting hares. Lamping therefore would not fall within this section but would be an offence under the general hunting with dogs law.

The offence can only be dealt with in the Magistrates Court and the penalty is a fine on Level 5

You can be arrested without a warrant for these offences.

Exempt Hunting

Certain activities are exempt. Stalking a wild mammal or flushing it out of cover are exempt if it is to prevent damage to the following: livestock, game birds or wild birds, food for livestock, crops, timber, fisheries, other property or the biological diversity of an area.

A hunt is exempt if it is to obtain meat for human or animal consumption or participation in a field trial.

In addition, hunting of rats and rabbits is exempt if it takes place on the hunter's land or on land the hunter has permission to use.

Protection of Badgers

Badgers are protected by law and it is an offence to wilfully kill, injure or take a badger or attempt to do any of those things. The section in relation to attempting is one of those cases where the burden of proof shifts. If the prosecution establish evidence from which it could be reasonably concluded that the person was attempting to commit one of those offences it shall be presumed he was attempting to commit one of those offences unless the contrary is shown. It would therefore fall to you to satisfy the Magistrates on the balance of probabilities that you were not attempting to commit an offence

The case can only be dealt with in the Magistrates Court but carries a maximum sentence of 6 months imprisonment or a Level 5 fine

It is also an offence to cruelly ill-treat a badger, dig for a badger or use badger tongs in the course of killing or taking or attempting to kill or take. There are also restrictions on the type of firearm which may be used.

Again the burden of proof is reversed in the same way as it is for attempts

Interfering with a badger sett in the following ways – damaging it or part of it, destroying it, obstructing access to it, causing a dog to enter it or disturbing a badger when it is occupying a sett are also offences if you intend to do those acts or are reckless as to whether your acts would have those consequences. An example of the latter would be to commence digging to lay foundations for a building which is close to a sett, and knowing the sett is there carry on regardless of the fact that you may interfere with the sett.

These offences can only be dealt with in the Magistrates Court but carry a maximum sentence of 6 months imprisonment or a Level 5 fine. However if you use a dog or a dog was present at the time the offence was committed the court MAY order for the destruction or other disposal of the dog or disqualify the offender from having custody of a dog. Note NOT 'own', simply 'custody'.

It is a defence to interfering with a sett to show that your actions were necessary to prevent serious damage to land, crops, poultry or another form of property.

The question you are probably asking yourself is what are the implications if your dog goes to ground and you are trying to retrieve it? If you try and dig your dog out you will almost certainly be prosecuted. It may be that you could try and avail yourself of the defence above asserting that your dog is property and you are preventing serious damage to it either from the badger attacking it or by leaving it there where it will die (and therefore be damaged). I would advise contacting the local wildlife officer for advice, it may be that if you can use a heat locator the dog may have escaped into a warren belonging to another animal. DO NOT DIG until you have consulted someone.

If it is a fox den or rabbit warren and you are sure of this then you can dig, again I would advise contacting your local wildlife officer for advice BEFORE you start digging as it is possible you will be reported if someone thinks it is a sett. Further I would advise you take photographs of the area so you can establish that IT IS NOT a sett.

Sheep worrying

Although commonly called 'sheep' worrying, it actually applies to livestock and this includes horses, mules, sheep, goats and swine.

Worrying means chasing in such a way as may be reasonably expected to cause injury or suffering. This includes, for females, causing miscarriage or for there to be fewer offspring.

It encompasses being at large, that is not on a lead or under close control in a field in which there are sheep. As emphasised before, if you cannot bring your dog to heel it is likely, if you are in a field of sheep, that you will be committing an offence EVEN if the dog does nothing. It is a defence if your dog is with someone else who you reasonably believed was a fit and proper person.

If you are convicted you can be fined at Level 3.

It is important to note that there is no reference in the Dogs (Protection of Livestock) Act 1953 regarding destruction or control of your dog, however there is a residual power from the Dogs Act 1906 which allows for a dog which is proved to have injured cattle or chased sheep to be dealt with as a dangerous dog under the 1871 Act. This means that a court may make an order for destruction or for a dog to be kept under control.

Miscellaneous offences

You may also be prosecuted if you are involved in an incident and you use your dog as a weapon.

If you remember Bill Sikes and his dog Bulls-Eye from the film 'Oliver', you will recollect that Bill used his dog to intimidate other people, effectively using it as a weapon. In such circumstances you may be guilty of offences of public order or assault. Every case will fall be decided on its own facts so I do not propose to examine them in depth.

Briefly, if a dog is used to attack someone and injury is caused they may be guilty of an assault. Assaults can be very minor, from a scratch to more serious life threatening injuries and the level of charge will be substantially determined by that. The prosecution will have to prove that the dog was used as a weapon, that is to say the owner in some ways caused or encouraged the dog to attack for example, the classic 'sic 'em' comment.

Similarly it the dog is used to threaten, the owner may be guilty of one of five offences under the Public Order Act 1986. Again it will be for the prosecution to establish that the owner was using the dog to threaten or intimidate.

Fraud

The Fraud Act 2006 covers those scenarios which we may refer to as a 'con' i.e. situations where you dupe or are duped. You will be guilty of an offence of fraud if you make false representation or by failing to disclose information or by abusing your position. You must do these acts dishonestly and with an intent to make a gain for yourself or cause another to lose or be at risk of loss.

Clearly this may involve dogs. For example if you sell a dog as pedigree and it isn't you may be guilty of an offence if you were dishonest about the pedigree and did it to make money. It is unlikely that the third type of offence will apply as that requires you to be in a position where you are expected to safeguard the financial interests of another, such as acting as a trustee.

Summary

It is not just dangerous dogs you have to worry about. There are numerous ways you may end up before the criminal court as a defendant or a victim.

CHAPTER FIVE
IRRESPONSIBLE DOG OWNERS: OTHER WAYS THE LAW GETS INVOLVED

This Chapter examines other ways in which the law intervenes to control dogs and their owners. In particular, the powers given to Local Authorities and others to control anti-social behaviour by dog owners.

Although many people in the community and some dog owners look to the criminal law as a means of enforcing responsible behaviour in dog owners since the introduction the Anti-Social Behaviour, Crime and Policing Act 2014, there are a whole raft of measures which can be used before the criminal law is invoked.

Under the Act, DEFRA published *'Dealing with irresponsible dog ownership: practitioners'* manual. Its aim is to 'encourage responsible dog ownership and reduce other incidents involving dogs such as straying and the use of dogs for intimidation, through early engagement and education, and overall to prevent problems becoming more serious and thus reduce the number of dog bites'.

Most people are aware that councils have dog wardens the police also have specialist officers called Dog Legislation Officer who's responsibilities include dangerous dogs and irresponsible owners

This can be achieved in several ways. Often the first step where an incident has occurred is that upon investigating the police may conclude that the best way forward is to invite the owner to enter into an Acceptable Behaviour Contract. Although this uses the term 'contract' it isn't a contract in the legal sense, but rather an agreement. The owner is invited to co-operate in measures to safeguard the public from any other incidents involving their dog. An example might be to muzzle your dog when in public spaces and to always have it on a lead. If such an order is breached there is no penalty, however if your dog is involved in an incident when the measures were not in place that may be used as evidence in a future court case. Such agreements are frequently used where the owner is engaging with the police and no other action is considered appropriate.

Community Protection Notice

Part 4 of the act permits authorised persons to issue a Community Protection Notice where the behaviour of the person is having a detrimental effect of a persistent or continuing nature on the quality of life of those in the locality and the behaviour is unreasonable. As well as police officers, authorised persons can be from the local authority and social landlords.

The behaviour could include persistent barking or an animal showing aggression to persons where the owner does nothing to prevent it.

Before a notice can be issued, a letter must be sent informing the owner of the problem and giving them an opportunity to stop the behaviour whilst also explaining what may happen if the problem persists.

If a CPN is issued it may require a person to stop doing certain things or require them to do certain things or take reasonable steps to achieve that result. This may mean muzzle a dog or keep it on a lead or require the owner to attend training class. Other examples are that the dog is only walked at certain times or excluded from certain areas. This is simply a list of examples. The notice should target the behaviour that is causing the problem, for example a requirement to muzzle a dog where the issue is that it strays from its garden. Here I would suggest the better requirement is to ensure the garden is properly enclosed.

If you are given a CPN you may challenge it by appealing to the magistrates court. You can only do this if you can show that the behaviour alleged did not occur, that it wasn't persistent or it didn't interfere with the quality of life, that it wasn't unreasonable or that it isn't behaviour that you can control. If you wish to challenge the CPN you must do so within 21 days of being served with it.

If you accept the CPN but then breach it there are two options open. The officer may decide to issue you with a Fixed Penalty Notice or prosecute you. The penalty is a fine at Level 4.

It is important to remember that section 50 of the Act gives the officer the right to seize any article used in the commission of the offence and dispose of it or destroy it, this could be your dog. Clearly this is a huge step and the guide suggests that seizing a dog is a significant step and should be carefully considered.

CPNs can only be given to persons over 16 years old.

Injunctions

Part 1 of the Act contains provision to apply for an injunction against a person engaging in or threatening to engage in anti-social behaviour and the court considers it to be just and convenient to make the order for the purpose of preventing the person from engaging in the behaviour.

The difference between CPN and injunctions is that to obtain an injunction the person requiring one must go to court to do so. An injunction can be made against a person over 10 years of age. There is no power to seize articles upon breach.

A variety of authorities can apply and these include the police, local authorities and social landlords.

You may challenge the making of an order. The court can only grant an order if it is satisfied on the balance of probabilities, more likely than not, that the person has engaged or threatened to engage in anti-social behaviour. An injunction must not interfere with your work or schooling

The aim of the injunction, similar to the CPN, is to prevent the behaviour complained of and it may contain prohibitions or requirements similar to a CPN. Clearly there is an overlap here, however an injunction may contain a power of arrest or the person supervising it may seek a warrant to arrest you. This means you may be arrested for breaching it.

If it is suspected you have breached an injunction you may be taken back to court. The court treat such a breach as contempt of court which is a serious matter. If you are over 18 years of age it carries a maximum sentence of 2 years. For someone under 18 the court may impose a youth supervision or in very serious cases detention and training order.

Criminal Behaviour Orders

Unlike the other two orders, a CBO can only be obtained if you are convicted of a criminal offence. They must be applied for at the time you are sentenced for the offence and similar to the other orders may contain prohibitions.

Public Space Protection Orders

Part 4 of the Act introduced Public Space Protection Orders (PSPOs). These orders are to protect places and rather than prohibiting one person they apply to a class of people in a restricted area. They are designed to prohibit anti-social behaviour, for example to prevent groups of youths gathering together. They are a replacement to the previous Dog Control Orders (DCOs).

PSPOs can only be issued by a local authority if activities carried on in that area are having a detrimental effect on the quality of life in the locality, the same as for a CPN, or it is likely that activities will be carried on in a public place that have that effect. In addition, the activity is likely to be of a persistent or continuing nature or is likely to be such as to be unreasonable. A PSPO must identify the area it refers to and the class of people and can either prohibit types of behaviour or require persons in that area to do specific things. The former may prohibit dogs from an area whilst the second may require a dog to be on a lead. It is also suggested that it may limit the number of dogs one person can walk at a time. The guide suggests this may be six, but in imposing such a restriction other factors may be taken into account, for example if the area includes a place where children frequent, in which case it may be lower.

Prior to making an order, the Local Authority must consult with the police, any landowners affected and such community representatives as it thinks appropriate. In relation to dogs this may include the Kennel Club, local vets, dog societies and animal welfare organisations. The list is a guide only. Best practice suggests that Local Authorities should advertise in the local press but there is no legal requirement for them to do so.

If you are in breach of a PSPO you may be issued with a fixed penalty ticket or prosecuted and fined to a maximum at Level 3.

Dog Control Orders

Any DCOs in existence at the time of the Act being introduced had to be reviewed within three years and if they are to remain will convert to PSPOs. As the Act commenced on 20th October 2014 all DCOs should have been reviewed and if necessary converted or shortly will be.

Summary

Local Authorities and others have the power to restrict how you interact with your dog in public. Failure to follow any restrictions may lead to a convictions and in the case of a CPN may lead to your dog being seized.

CHAPTER SIX
THE DOG IN YOUR HOME: EVEN HERE THE LAW MAY GET YOU

This chapter is designed to look at issues which may arise with your dog at home. It deals with issues which may be considered to be part of the civil rather than the criminal law. Some of the behaviour may be categorised as a 'nuisance' or 'negligence'.

Simply because you are in your own home does not mean that you have no responsibility to control your dog or their environment.

Nuisance

An example of nuisance may be barking, whilst negligence may be allowing your dog to hurt someone inside your home.

A nuisance, as applied to your dog at home, is if you keep your dog in such a way as to cause substantial annoyance and/or discomfort to the public, e.g. persistent barking. It may also cover keeping your dog in such condition that rats are present.

The remedy for anybody affected is to make a claim in the civil court for compensation and/or an injunction. This is a court order to stop you from allowing it to happen in the future.

Barking

All dogs bark but at some point the barking may become a nuisance and impact upon a neighbours enjoyment or use of their land. This may be an actionable as a nuisance, however it will depend upon the degree – it has to be substantial.

If your neighbour complains about persistent barking or barking late at night he may claim in the County Court for damages and/or an injunction. Damages are a sum of money designed to compensate your neighbour for the nuisance. More significantly he can ask for an injunction which is a court order designed to stop the nuisance. This may mean that you have to take steps to prevent your dog barking, such as undergoing training.

In addition, the Local Authority has power under the Environmental Protection Act 1990. They must investigate in any case where an animal is kept in such a place or manner as to be prejudicial to health or is a nuisance and if noise is emitted from premises as as to be prejudicial to heath or a nuisance. See section 79 (1) (f) & (g).

If a neighbour complains to the Local Authority about barking dogs it is usually dealt with as a noise pollution issue. To be considered as such it must unreasonable and substantially interfere with the use or enjoyment of the home OR injure or be likely to injure health. If the Local authority agree they are obliged to serve an Abatement Notice on you to stop the noise. The notice is a legal document and must give you a time limit in which to comply and it must inform you that if you fail you may be prosecuted.

It is possible for the Authority to delay serving a notice and try to find another solution; but this is only for 7 days.

Breach of Abatement Notice

If you are served with an Abatement Notice and fail without reasonable excuse to stop the noise the Local Authority may issue you with a Fixed Penalty Notice which usually will not exceed £110. The alternative is to prosecute you in the Magistrates Court. If you are convicted you may be fined up to a maximum of £5000, although the Magistrates may also add a further $1/10^{th}$ of the maximum for every day the nuisance continues up to an absolute maximum of £20000 and this may be ongoing. It is important to note that it must be without reasonable excuse. Potentially if you are seeking help to train your dog, because of separation anxiety as an example, but it has not yet been completed, you may have a defence.

Another form of nuisance may be as a result of the conditions your dog lives in. For example if faeces are not cleaned up and the smell becomes a problem for your neighbours, or the condition you keep your dogs in attracts vermin.

In both of these situations the Local Environmental Health officer may become involved.

Negligence

Injury to others

Under the civil law an occupier of premises may be responsible for injury/damage caused to a person within the premises occupied. This is covered by the Occupiers Liability Act 1957. First thing to note is that it applies to an occupier not an owner. That is to say it applies to a person *who has sufficient degree of control over premises to put him under a duty of care towards those who are lawfully upon the premises.*

Persons lawfully upon your premises may include a person coming to your front door to post a leaflet or it may be your grandchildren. To these people under the Act you owe a duty of care that is to say 'a duty to take such care as in all the circumstances of the case is reasonable'.

If this happened the person injured may sue for damages.

Two examples: If for example you have an excitable dog who bites the postie whilst on your property he or she or even their employer on their behalf may take action against you for compensation. In some circumstances the Post Office may refuse to deliver your mail.

Warning notices do not necessarily *release* you from liability unless it is sufficient in all the circumstances of the case and in fact may make matters worse. For example if you have a notice which implies you have a dangerous dog it may.

You do not owe a duty of care to trespassers

Of course as referred to earlier the criminal law concerning dangerousness now applies inside private properties as well.

Escape

Unless you can be absolutely sure your dogs will not stray off your property it is always best to have them enclosed. You have a statutory obligation to prevent your animals, including dogs from straying onto the highway. Section 8 Animals Act 1971 reversed the common law rules of negligence which restricted or excluded liability to take reasonable care to prevent damage caused to road users by animals straying onto the highway. You must therefore take steps to prevent your dog straying onto the highway and causing an accident involving cars, bicycles and pedestrians.

As is common in many situations, what is reasonable will depend on the facts of each case. It does not place an absolute duty. This means your fence etc doesn't have to be 100% secure, simply reasonably adequate to prevent escape. Factors which may be taken into account may include the type of fencing, gate or other security use, how close to the Highway the land is and how busy the highway is. That is to say the busier the road the more secure you should be.

If your dog does escape and causes a road traffic collision you may be sued in the civil courts for any damage to vehicles or personal injuries caused.

Summary

Even inside your home or own land you still have a duty to ensure you have your dog under control so that it doesn't cause annoyance to your neighbours or injure a visitor. In addition you must ensure that your dog cannot escape from your property and cause damage.

CHAPTER SEVEN
THE DOG OUTSIDE YOUR HOME: THE PERILS OF OUTSIDE

In this chapter I will look at the many problems surrounding dogs whilst away from your home. There are a number of situations of which you need to be aware which may place you in trouble, but also endanger your dog, including how you interact with other road users and how you use public places.

The Highway Code has guidance on a number of issues which affect dog owners. For example the guidance at Rule 57 is not to let a dog out on the road on its own and to keep it on a short lead on pavements roads or paths that are shared with cyclists or horses. Remember that although much of the Highway Code is for guidance, any breach of a rule may be relied on in any court (civil or criminal) to support an allegation.

Other Road Users: Cyclists

The thorny issue of cyclists and dogs on footpaths! If you are on a traditional path, cyclists are prohibited from riding on them (Rule 64). The issues arise when there is a dual cycle and pedestrian path.

Rule 62 provides for two categories of cycle track: Segregated and Unsegregated.

A segregated path will have a blue circular sign with a pedestrian and cyclist side by side separated by a white line. This sign means that part of the path is a formally designated footpath whilst the other is for cyclists to use. If your dog strays into the opposing path and causes a cyclist to fall you may be liable for damage.

An unsegregated path can be identified by a blue circular sign with a cyclist above a pedestrian. This is a shared route and care must be exercised by both pedestrians and dogs.

On both routes however, caution should be exercised. Remember Rule 56!

Segregated route for pedal cycles and pedestrians

Shared route for pedal cycles and pedestrians

Pedestrians

Many people are happy to see you and your dog, however you must take care and remember not everyone is a dog lover! Always bear in mind Rule 56!

Section 2 of the Animals Act 1971 provides that the keeper of an animal which is not a dangerous species (this includes dogs) is liable for damage caused by them in the following situations:

- The damage caused or likely to be caused is severe.

- The dog has characteristics not normally found in a dog.

- You are aware of those characteristics.

For example, if you have a dog which you know has a propensity to attack another dog, attacks another dog and the owner is injured you will be liable for damages to the owner.

You can escape liability if the damage is the fault of the person injured, they accepted the risk or if the person is trespassing on your property.

That is not the end of the story. Someone may also sue you using the general principles of negligence referred to in Chapter 5. You have a duty as a dog owner to other people when you are out to take reasonable care to avoid an act or omission which you can reasonably foresee would be likely to cause damage to another.

An example might be; if your dog was off its lead and it jumped up at an elderly person who was hurt as a result. You as a reasonable dog owner may be liable for damages if it was reasonable for you to foresee damage or injury occurring to another person if your dog is off its lead.

A note of caution – just because your dog is on a lead does not absolve you from responsibility. You may be responsible under the above example where your dog is on its lead but you don't have control of it.

Similarly, be aware of extending leads. If not monitored properly and your dog runs in front of a cyclist, you may be liable as well.

Whilst legislation mentioned in Chapters Three and Four which refer to criminal acts, you may also be responsible under the two preceding paragraphs for harm caused to another animal such as a dog.

The Countryside

The most important factor to remember when in the countryside, especially near livestock, is your responsibility to keep proper control of your dog.

Under the civil law, Section 3 Animals Act 1971 makes the keeper of a dog liable for any damage caused by killing or injuring any livestock. It is also an offence under section 1 Dogs (Protection of Livestock) Act 1953 if your dog worries livestock. Note that livestock includes not just sheep and cows but extends to poultry, goats and horses. Worrying includes chasing as well as attacking if in such a way as may be reasonably expected to cause injury. Importantly it includes your dog being at large — that is not on a lead or under close control, if in a field or enclosure in which there are sheep. If your dog is being walked by someone else they may be convicted. It is a defence for you to show that the dog was in the charge of some person you reasonably believed to be a fit and proper person. The penalty if you are convicted is a fine.

Be aware that you may also be prosecuted for offences under the Dangerous Dogs Act 1991 and complaints made under the Dogs Act 1871 which opens up the possibility of destruction of your dog.

It is important to note therefore that the livestock does not have to be on land owned by the owner of the stock, the protection extends to livestock on unfenced land such as a moor where the owner has a right to graze.

Most importantly an owner may shoot your dog if it is worrying sheep.

Open Access Land

In 2000 the restrictive laws in relation to rights of access in the countryside underwent a substantial change with the introduction of the Countryside and Public Rights of Way Act. Since then under section 2 of the act people have been entitled to enjoy certain areas, as set out on a map, without restriction as long as they do not break or damage any wall hedge, fence, gate or stile. There are further restrictions set out in Schedule 2 such as lighting fires or using a metal detector.

I mention it here because it does impact on dog owners by the imposition of restrictions. Schedule 2 of the act places restrictions in relation to the period 31st March to 1st July when all dogs must be kept on a short lead. Further a dog must be on a short lead when in the vicinity of livestock. Livestock refers to cattle and sheep, swine and poultry.

Further if the land is a moor managed for the breeding and shooting of grouse and it appears necessary for the proper management of the land a landowner may impose further restrictions under section 23. The maximum period the restriction may apply is 5 years. Finally a landowner may prohibit dogs from any field or enclosure in which there are sheep for one 6 week period in a year.

Beaches

Many beaches or parts of them are now closed to dogs during summer periods. It is not possible to list them all here as they tend to be dealt with by local bylaws. Be vigilant as the signs are posted.

Hotels, cafes, restaurants, shops and pubs

The exclusion of dogs from any building is at the discretion of the owner/manager. It is a myth that dogs are by law excluded from premises selling food because of health and safety.

There are regulations made under the Food Safety Act 1990 which impose a duty for the premises owner to ensure there are adequate precautions in place to ensure that access to a place where food is prepared, handled or stored is denied to dogs (and other animals).

You can legally take your dog into a pub but it will be a breach of the Food Standards regulations if your dog goes into the kitchen. This is the responsibility of the owner and could be why many simply ban pets as it is easier.

You are entitled to point this out politely and ask them to change the policy but be prepared for a 'no'!

Also be aware that if you are allowed entry the owner/manager is entitled to ask you to leave if your dog becomes unruly in any way.

Other places may also place a restriction, such as DIY stores, but again this is a policy matter and not a legal obligation.

The Equality Act 2010 makes it unlawful for a person to be discriminated against because they have a disability. This includes excluding people from premises because they have an assistance dog with them. Therefore pubs etc. cannot refuse you entry because you have a guide dog for example.

Summary

Beware of other road users and be considerate towards them. There is no legal duty for you to be excluded from any premises, this is entirely up to the owner of the premises. If you are allowed access keep your dog under control or you may be excluded. If you have a dog to assist with a disability you cannot be excluded.

CHAPTER EIGHT
TRAVELLING WITH YOUR DOG: BUSES, PLANES, TRAINS AND AUTOMOBILES

In this Chapter I look at the law regarding travelling with your dog, the pitfalls you should look out for and the possible consequences. It includes your dog in the car, pet passports and using ferries, trains and planes.

<u>The Car</u>

The most frequent journey you will make with your dog is likely to be in the car. The guidance in the Highway Code Rule 57 recommends that a dog should be 'suitably restrained' whilst in a car; it gives examples of using a seat belt restraint or a crate. The explanation it gives is to prevent distraction or injury to yourself or the dog.

It is not difficult to understand why this is important. There is potential, if you are distracted by your dog momentarily, that you could be guilty of the offence of driving without due care and attention which simply requires a momentary lapse in concentration for you to be guilty. Such an offence carries a financial penalty and penalty points.

The more serious offence of Dangerous Driving carries a term of imprisonment as a penalty and if someone is killed it is a maximum of 10 years. To be guilty of this offence your standard of driving must fall well below that of a competent and careful driver and it is obvious to a competent and careful driver that driving in that way would be dangerous. It may be that if you are aware that you have an unruly dog who cannot remain still, for example persistently trying to climb from the back to the front of your car, and you are then involved in a collision.

In relation to car travel, and most other travel, it is worth checking the position in relation to your car insurance and your breakdown cover before you travel. Check whether you are covered for loss or injury to your animal, you should be because it is a possession. The more serious issue is breakdown assistance. It is common for breakdown/recovery companies to reserve the right not to transport an animal. Unfortunately it may well be that you don't know until the van arrives, especially if the service has been sent to an agency. Some recovery firms will not permit dogs to travel in a cab, which may be understandable, if the animal cannot be restrained. They may insist on your dog travelling in your car. It is common for insurance companies to reserve the right not to transport an animal.

Trains

Dogs are allowed on trains, again at the discretion of the operator. There may be restrictions on your travel. Your dog should be on a lead on in a carrier. You should certainly should never allow your dog on the seats. If your dog becomes unruly you may be asked to move or even leave the train.

In addition, in any travel you need to ensure that your dog is comfortable. Ensure you have sufficient water and or food for your dog. If you are travelling a long distance consider whether to break your journey to allow your dog to stretch his legs and relieve himself.

Traveling Abroad and Returning to the UK

Pet Passports

In effect this is a certificate to show that your dog is fit and healthy and able to travel. As the dog is tracked using its microchip the first step is to ensure the dog is microchipped (remember it is now compulsory). I would also advise that it is checked and found to be functioning and in the same position it was implanted. If not, record where it is.

Your dog must be vaccinated against rabies and tapeworm. The rabies vaccine must be administered at least 21 days before your return to ensure it is effective, Tapeworm protection must be administered no less than 24 hours and no more than 120 hours before you enter the UK.

Both of these must be administered by a vet and certified as such by a vet.

Eurotunnel – you can use the tunnel and the train service to transport your animal.

Ferries

Ferries are also regulated for the bringing in of pets to the UK and Defra has a full list. The main ferry operators such as P&O and DFDS are regulated. There are also restrictions on which ports/routes you can use.

It is advisable to make arrangements well in advance as usually there are only a limited number of pet friendly cabins available and if you miss out you may have to leave your dog in the car.

Foot passengers are generally allowed to be accompanied by their dog but it is advisable to check.

Planes

Travelling on a plane with your dog can be complicated as there are a variety of air carriers with different policies, for example some won't carry snub nosed dogs such as pugs because of difficulties with breathing at altitude. The best advice is to use a specialist 'travel agent' to make the arrangements for you. They can advise on the requirements for the country you are entering and leaving.

If you are returning or entering the UK with your dog you must use certain airports and airlines which are regulated to handle animals. Most of the larger airports are regulated such as Heathrow, Gatwick, Manchester, Edinburgh, and many smaller local airports such as Robin Hood and Bristol are regulated. A full list is available from the Defra website. You can also use a charter flight into certain private airports. Again it is best to check the Defra website for a full list.

Certain airlines are registered to carry pets onboard in the cabin, subject to certain restrictions. Others are registered to carry them only in the hold. This will often depend on the size of your pet and you should check before you make a booking.

Summary

Travel with any pet is not easy and you need to take care even on short journeys in the car in the UK. The rules above give guidance about travelling with ferries and planes abroad and the restrictions on how and when you can return into the UK with your dog.

CHAPTER NINE
ANIMAL WELFARE: LOOKING AFTER YOUR DOG

In this chapter I look at the issue of animal welfare. This include a will look at the Animal Welfare Act 2006 plus other issues of welfare not in the act such as kennels, breeding establishments and home boarding. Finally, the issue of notifiable diseases.

The Animal Welfare Act lays out general rules of welfare and offences as a result of failure to follow the rules. These are all relevant to dog owners The Act sets out in 4 parts the responsibilities and prohibitions under the law. It also deals with who is responsible for enforcing the act and the powers they may have for seizing an animal and power of arrest.

<u>Prevention of Harm</u>

These sections set out general provisions as to suffering to animals or mutilation of animals.

Section 4 makes it an offence if, by an act or failure to act, a person causes an animal to suffer. In order to be guilty of an offence the person must know or ought reasonably to have known that the act or failure to act would have that effect and that the suffering is unnecessary.

It is not only an owner who may be guilty but any 'person responsible for the animal'. This includes people who are responsible on a temporary basis, such as a dog sitter or friend caring for an animal, or a person who is in charge of the animal.

In deciding whether the suffering was unnecessary the act sets out a list of considerations which are relevant. This is not an exhaustive list which means the court can look at other factors. The list – could the suffering reasonably have been avoided or reduced; was the suffering in compliance with any relevant enactment; was the suffering for a legitimate purpose, such as the purpose of benefitting the animal or protecting a person, property or another animal; was the suffering proportionate; was the conduct that of a reasonably competent and humane person

This is a wide-ranging section and may cover anything from failing to seek vetinary treatment to actual harm, for example attempting to euthanise a dog in such a way as to cause distress to the animal.

A person will be guilty if they had knowledge of the suffering or should have been aware. This latter captures the common situation where it is obvious that an animal is suffering but the person responsible seems not to realise it.

Section 5 prohibits mutilation of animals and makes it an offence to carry out a prohibited procedure or causes a prohibited procedure to be carried out. Again an offence is committed by the person responsible for the animal if they allowed another person to carry out the procedure and permitted or failed to stop the procedure.

A prohibited procedure involves interference with the sensitive tissues or bone structure of the animal otherwise than for medical treatment.

Clearly this section is aimed at non vets carrying out surgery on an animal such as castration.

Section 6 makes it an offence to dock a dogs tail whether in part or whole save for the purpose of medical treatment. As a person responsible for a dog you will guilty of an offence if you permit someone to remove a tail or fail to prevent it and to show a dog at an event where the public pay to be admitted, unless it is being shown to demonstrate its working ability only.

It is permitted under The Docking of Working Dogs Tails (England) Regulations 2007 to dock a dog where it is to be used in law enforcement, the armed forces, emergency rescue, lawful pest control or the lawful shooting of animals IF it is a hunt point retrieve breed, a spaniel breed or a terrier breed or combination. The dog must be certified as a working dog before it is 5 days old. This must be by a vet who has to see specific information produced to him in writing. There are similar regulations in Wales and Northern Ireland.

Section 7 makes it an offence to poison a dog if it is done without reasonable excuse or lawful authority. In addition the person must know that it is a poisonous or injurious. Again, a responsible person will be guilty if they permit or culpably fail to prevent the administration of a poison. In addition it is an offence to causes any such substance to be taken by a dog.

Section 8 outlaws dog fighting in the following ways – by causing or attempting to cause a dog fight, that is to say arrange the fight; by receiving money for admission to a dog fight; by publicising a dog fight; by providing information to another about a dog fight in order to encourage them to attend; by making a bet on the outcome; by taking part in a dog fight; by having in his possession anything designed or adapted for use in connection with a dog fight with the intention of it so being used; by keeping or training an animal for use in connection with an animal fight;or by keeping premises for the use of an animal fight.

Items designed or adapted may be lamps or fencing or corralling material.

In addition, it is an offence to be present at a fight. It is also an offence to possess, show, publish or supply a video of an animal fight.

An animal fight is where a protected animal is placed with an animal or with a human for the purpose of fighting, wrestling or baiting. In order to be an animal fight the word 'places' suggests some measure of control and restraint. For example taking lurches out into the countryside in the hope they will scare up an animal such as a fox, deer, badger for there to be a pursuit and fight when the wild animal is cornered is not an animal fight. It might be something. However, encircling a space with onlookers and putting animals in to fight may be an animal fight.

All the above offences carry a term of imprisonment of 51 weeks if a person is convicted and/or a fine of £20,000. There is pressure being brought by welfare organisations to demand an increase in the penalty.

Promotion of Welfare

As it says, the next sections of the Act deal with the promotion of welfare of animals.

Section 9 places a duty on a person to take reasonable steps to ensure that the needs of an animal are met. An animal's needs include: a suitable environment and diet; an ability to exhibit normal behaviour patterns; any need to house it with or apart from other animals; to protect it from pain, suffering, injury and disease. There is no specific reference here as to the mental wellbeing of an animal although it may be that being able to exhibit normal behaviour patterns would cover it. It is arguable therefore that a dog which is otherwise well cared for, but is an outside animal with little interaction with an owner is not covered by this offence, although if its faeces are not removed it will be.

It is clear there is an overlap with Section 4 and preventing unnecessary suffering. The major difference is in the enforcement, whilst section 9 makes it a criminal offence, it also allows for intervention by the RSPCA.

Section 10 permits an inspector to serve an improvement notice on a person who is failing to comply with section 9. The notice must state that the inspector is of the opinion the person is failing and the ways in which he is failing, the steps the inspector considers need to be taken to comply with the section, the period for compliance and the consequences of failing to comply.

Section 11 is a curious section and makes it an offence to sell an animal to a person under 16. See the commentary in relation to young people walking dogs. This will also include the chance to win an animal as a prize.

Under the Act there is provision for the issue of Codes of Practice providing practical guidance in relation to any of the above sections. A failure to comply with any code is not an offence but may be used as tending to establish liability in the same way the highway code is used. DEFRA (Department for Environmental and Rural Affairs) has published guidance on dogs.

The penalty for offences under this part is imprisonment of 51 weeks or a level 5 fine.

Available Powers

Section 18 permits an inspector or a police officer to take such steps as are reasonably necessary to alleviate an animal's suffering. Importantly this section does not give authority to destroy an animal unless a veterinary surgeon certifies that the condition of the animal is such that it should be destroyed in its own interests. However an inspector or constable MAY destroy an animal without a certificate IF there is no reasonable alternative to destroying it AND it is not reasonably practicable to wait for a vet..

In addition, the inspector or police officer may take possession of an animal where the veterinary surgeon certifies that it is suffering or it is likely to suffer if its circumstances do not change. Again the inspector can act without the vet if it is not reasonably practicable to wait.

If the animal is taken into possession it may be removed to a place of safety.

It is an offence to deliberately obstruct a person exercising powers under this section.

In addition, a police officer may seize an animal it it appears to him that it is involved in dog fighting.

A warrant may be issued by a Magistrates court to enter premises.

Kennels

There are two distinct types of kennel – the Boarding Kennel and the Breeding Kennel. As well as being regulated by the Animal Welfare Act, if you are involved in running either you are subject to additional regulation.

Boarding Kennels

Boarding Kennels are subject to regulation under the Animal Boarding Establishments Act 1963. The basic requirement is to have a licence granted by your local authority.

In granting a licence the Local Authority will look at the following factors and may impose conditions on the licence to ensure they are met. The accommodation the animal is kept in. It must be of the correct size for the animal or the number of animals with adequate light, temperature and ventilation and exercise facilities.

Further, you will have to demonstrate that the animals are given suitable food, drink and bedding material,; that it is adequately exercised and is visited at suitable intervals.

You must have in place reasonable precautions to prevent the spread of infectious disease and if necessary have isolation facilities available. In addition you must take appropriate steps in case of emergency.

Finally that you keep a register of the animals coming and leaving and the name and address of owners.

You must allow your premises to be inspected. Failure to have a licence is a criminal offence. Your licence may be cancelled and you may be disqualified from keeping kennels for such a period as the court thinks fit.

A boarding establishment is quite widely defined. It includes carrying on at premises a business of providing other people's animals with accommodation. This includes dwelling houses.

You do not need a licence if you accommodate other people's animals as part of a business but the provision of accommodation is not the main activity. The regulations will apply to businesses that offer dog walking and sitting services but not to a vet who accommodates an animal during treatment.

Breeding Kennels or Establishments

The Breeding of Dogs Act 1973 regulates breeding establishments or kennels. As many now breed from their own dogs I will first look at the definition of a Breeding Establishment before looking at the law regulating them.

Section 4A of the Act defines an establishment

> *'A person keeps a breeding establishment for dogs at any premises if he carries on at those premises a business of breeding dogs for sale (whether by him or any other person).*
>
> *(3) Subject to subsection (5) of this section, where—*
>
> *(a) a person keeps a bitch at any premises at any time during any period of twelve months; and*
>
> *(b) the bitch gives birth to a litter of puppies at any time during that period,*
>
> *he shall be treated as carrying on a business of breeding dogs for sale at the premises throughout the period if a total of four or more other litters is born during the period to bitches falling within subsection (4) of this section.*

(4) The bitches falling within this subsection are—

(a) the bitch mentioned in subsection (3)(a) and (b) of this section and any other bitches kept by the person at the premises at any time during the period;

(b) any bitches kept by any relative of his at the premises at any such time;

(c) any bitches kept by him elsewhere at any such time; and

(d) any bitches kept (anywhere) by any person at any such time under a breeding arrangement made with him.

(5) Subsection (3) of this section does not apply if the person shows that none of the puppies born to bitches falling within paragraph (a), (b) or (d) of subsection (4) of this section was in fact sold during the period (whether by him or any other person).

(6) In subsection (4) of this section " breeding arrangement " means a contract or other arrangement under which the person agrees that another person may keep a bitch of his on terms that, should the bitch give birth, the other person is to provide him with either—

(a) one or more of the puppies; or

(b) the whole or part of the proceeds of selling any of them;

and "relative" means the person's parent or grandparent, child or grandchild, sibling, aunt or uncle or niece or nephew or someone with whom he lives as a couple.'

The guidance from DEFRA refers to non-business breeders as 'hobby breeders' who are people who do not have more than 5 litters in a year. I suspect some of you out there will be affronted by the terminology but it is simply to differentiate you from those who carry out breeding as a business or occupation.

If you fall within the definition you need to obtain a licence form your Local Authority which will consider it on similar lines to the boarding establishment, i.e. provision of quarters, food and water, light and prevention of spread of disease. In particular the Authority are required to have regard to the age of any bitch and it suggests that a licence may not be granted if a bitch is mated when under 1 year of age, they do not have more than one litter a year, or six litters in total.

It is a criminal offence if you have a breeding establishment without a licence or obstruct any person inspecting the premises. You may be fined, your licence revoked and disqualified from holding a licence and having custody of a dog.

Pet Shops

Although there is a growing trend away from selling dogs in pet shops it is still legal. Under the Pet Animals Act 1971 a pet shop is defined as carrying on business, from any premises, of buying and selling animals as pets. This includes from a home. You do not operate a pet shop if you keep or sell a pedigree dog bred by you or the offspring of a dog you keep as a pet.

If you fall within the definition you must hold a licence from your Local Authority. Similar factors to those referred to above for breeding and boarding establishments are taken into account in granting a licence. If you fail to have a licence you may be committing a criminal offence for which you may be fined at Level 2.

It is also a requirement that you allow the premises to be inspected and it is a criminal offence to wilfully obstruct any person trying to do this. This is also a criminal offence for which you may be fined at Level 2.

In addition, Section 2 of the Act makes It is illegal to carry on a business of buying and selling animals from a barrow or stall in a street, road or public place.

Notifiable diseases

There are a number of diseases under the law which are required to be notified to the Animal and Plant Health Agency and these diseases are the reason that the UK for so many years had strict quarantine laws for animals coming into the country. The main disease which is listed which you as a dog owner may come into contact with is rabies. You need to be aware that some diseases need to notify to the agency but your vet is the best person to assist if you suspect rabies or another serious disease.

Summary

The law makes provision to ensure all animals are treated in a fair and proper manner including the conditions in which they are kept by a private owner. In order to achieve this there are offences of animal cruelty and regulation of breeding, boarding and sale of animals.

CHAPTER TEN
END OF LIFE: TIME TO SAY GOODBYE

And so we arrive at the end. Although this is a sad subject I feel it is important to look at a couple of issues.

Your Death

The law has a part to play here. Your dog is a chattel and it is perfectly appropriate for you to make arrangements for your dog when you die. In fact I would urge you do to so.

The best way to do this is to make a will. As a chattel you can leave your dog to someone. This can be anyone you like and if you feel it is necessary you can leave a sum of money to that person on condition they take your dog and use the money for the benefit of the dog.

Charities

Many charities will take on a dog whose owner is deceased but usually you will need to arrange this prior to your passing and it may come with strings attached.

The Cinnamon Trust is one such which will assist you with walking and caring for and rehoming your pet after you have passed.

The RSPCA operate a home for life scheme which does what it says on the tin.

Both of the above require you to make arrangements before your death.

Your Dog Passing

Hopefully after a long life your dog will pass away peacefully in which case skip this section. You may take your dog to a vet to euthanise (put to sleep). This will be the least painful for your pet. Under the Animal Welfare Act if you choose to carry this out yourself you may be guilty of an offence either by carrying out a protected procedure or by causing unnecessary suffering, if, let's be honest, you botch it. My advice would always be to seek out professional help. There are charities who will assist you such as the PDSA, if you are short of funds.

If your pet passes at a vets it is still your property and you are entitled to remove it, you do not have to agree to the vet disposing of the remains that is a matter for you.

Pet Burials

Once again the law treats your dog as a chattel and once it has passed it is considered to be waste which is governed by Environmental Law. There are specialist companies who will arrange your pet burial or cremation. They are strictly governed by Environmental law, you don't need to worry about that. One thing you might be concerned about is what happens if the company ceases to operate, it may be that if buried in a pet cemetery you will no longer be able to visit.

Home Burials

You can bury your pet in your own garden. You must ensure that you bury it in such a position and deep enough that it does not constitute an environmental hazard, for example potentially contaminate a water source. There are guides available to assist with all the correct procedures.

You MUST NOT bury your dog in the garden if it would constitute a hazard, for example if it died from rabies.

One final note – once buried, you cannot dig your animal up. Think carefully about a home burial. If you sell, you cannot take your dog and it may be that it is something you have to disclose to a potential buyer.

Summary

Even as we say goodbye, the law has a part to play. Think carefully about how you want to dispose of your pet's remains. Once the decision is made it is difficult to change your mind.

CHAPTER ELEVEN
LEGAL PROCEDURES: IF IT ALL GOES WRONG

In this chapter I look at the legal procedures in both the criminal and county courts. It is by necessity a very brief overview in both cases.

Criminal Courts

The criminal courts are governed by a number of statues and operate under the Criminal Procedure Rules. The majority of criminal offences in the UK are prosecuted by the Crown Prosecution Service, although there are other bodies responsible for certain offences. The RSPCA are responsible for Animal Welfare and Local Authorities for breach of licences.

The decision to prosecute

Although an initial decision to prosecute may be made by the police, it is the Crown Prosecution Service who have the responsibility to prosecute cases in accordance with the Code for Crown Prosecutors (The Code).

It is perhaps important to note here that the CPS are not responsible for an investigation. The Code says 'The police and other investigators are responsible for conducting enquiries into any alleged crime and for deciding how to deploy their resources. This includes decisions to start or continue an investigation and on the scope of the investigation'.

If you are unhappy about a case not being investigated at all or appropriately it is a matter to take up with the police.

Before a case goes to court it will be reviewed in accordance with The Code for Crown Prosecutors. This involves two stages – the evidential test and the public interest test.

The evidential test requires the CPS to assess the evidence and determine if there is a reasonable prospect of conviction. This means – is there sufficient evidence which means it is more likely than not that a court will convict? It should be noted here that this is not the criminal standard of proof.

In deciding the above, the lawyer must look at all the evidence that is available. This includes looking at evidence which suggests the offence was not committed as well as evidence which does. They must look at any defence put forward, this will usually be taken from any interview. They must also look at how credible the evidence is and whether a court will admit it.

It is only if there is a realistic prospect of conviction that a lawyer will go on to the next stage. That is to say if there is not such a prospect the case must be stopped. It doesn't matter how serious it is.

The public interest test involves the lawyer considering a number of factors including: how serious is the offence; the

CHAPTER ELEVEN – LEGAL PROCEDURES: IF IT ALL GOES WRONG • 89

more serious it is the more likely it is that prosecution will follow; the impact on the victim.

One factor reads as follows:

> *Prosecutors should also consider whether prosecution is proportionate to the likely outcome, and in so doing the following may be relevant to the case under consideration:*
>
> *The cost to the CPS prosecution service and the wider criminal justice system, especially where it could be regarded as excessive when weighed against any likely penalty (Prosecutors should not decide the public interest on the basis of this factor alone. It is essential that regard is also given to the public interest factors identified when considering the other questions in paragraphs **4.12 a) to g)**, but cost is a relevant factor when making an overall assessment of the public interest).*

In this day and age economics come into all decisions so as we can see, although it is not a determinative factor, it is considered. If the penalty is likely to be minimal then prosecution is less likely. Obviously, under this heading however, the lawyer should have regard to whether or not the court will make a destruction order or a contingent destruction order. It may well be that if, having taken account of other factors that the low penalty including the fact a destruction will not be made, that a prosecution will not follow.

At Court

Your first appearance will be at the local Magistrates Court. At that appearance, or before if the CPS know your solicitor, you will receive basic information about the case against you. This could be a case summary or important witness statements. You will be asked to enter a plea of either 'Guilty' or 'Not Guilty'. If you have been charged with an aggravated offence, your case can be heard in the Crown Court. This is decided first by the Court. The general rule now is that a case should be heard by the Magistrates unless any sentence imposed upon conviction will clearly be outside the Magistrates powers. If the court decides they will hear it you still have the right to have your case heard by a Judge and Jury in the Crown Court. Always remember that such decisions on plea and where to have any trial have financial implications so need to be taken with a cool head.

If you plead guilty the court will go on to sentence you.

If you plead not guilty and the case stays in the Magistrates Court a date will be fixed for the court to hear the evidence and make a decision. If it goes to the Crown Court a date will be fixed for you to appear there and then a trial date. The trial will follow the same basic structure referred to below.

The Trial

Before the trial the CPS must serve on you all the evidence they are going to rely on. You can either accept it, in which case it will be read to court, or reject it. If it is the latter the

CPS must arrange for the witnesses to come to court to supply evidence and be cross examined by you or your lawyer.

It is for the prosecution to prove the case against you save in the circumstances referred to in the chapter on dangerous dogs (e.g. the assumption that the dog is a pit bull type). The court can only convict if they are satisfied so that they are sure of your guilt.

One situation that frequently arises is where you have been charged with a criminal offence under the Dangerous Dogs Act 1991 and also are before the court in relation to a complaint under The Dogs Act 1871. The problem which arises is that this a civil complaint and not a criminal offence, so the criminal rules do not apply, although some lawyers are not aware of this. The main difficulty is that any allegation under the Dogs Act only requires the court to think it is more likely than not that your dog is dangerous and under proper control. The concern is that the court confuses the two and applies the wrong standard.

Sentence

If you are convicted the court will go on to look at sentencing. This will be for you and the dog.

If it is a serious case a report, prepared by the Probation Service, may be ordered into your circumstances and recommending an appropriate sentence. I have already dealt with destruction orders in Chapter Three

Victims

The other time you will come into contact with the court is if you or your dog have been the victim of an offence. As you note from the wording of The Code it is for the police to investigate any crime. If you are not satisfied with their response you may wish to make a complaint. However it may be best to either go to an officer above the one you are dealing with or approach the force dog legislation officer.

If the case has been reviewed by the CPS and they decide at any stage not to proceed with the case you will be informed in writing. In some cases you may have been consulted first. If you are not happy with the decision you may ask for it to be reviewed.

The Civil Court Process

The Civil Courts, like the Criminal Courts, are governed by statutes and their own Civil Procedure Rules. The exact procedure you follow may vary according to the nature of your claim. I set out below a brief and standardized procedure.

Before commencing an action the Courts now require the parties, that is you and the person you are taking action against, to try and either settle before going to court or narrow down the issues. It may be that you can enter into a process called Alternative Dispute Resolution, usually mediation. This is aimed at therapies trying to come to a mutual agreement on how to settle the dispute. If you do reach an agreement and the other party fails to comply you can sue them for breach of the contract of agreement.

If you decide to make a claim you must fill in a claim form setting out your case. For example 'I was bitten by their dog on 1st January 2017'. The form requires you to state what you want, in particular the sum of money you are claiming. This figure will determine the actual route the claim follows. It is unlikely you can put an actual figure but you can limit to sue for example less than £10,000 or £10.000 to £25,000. You have to pay a fee to start the process and this will depend on the figure you claim.

Once you have completed the form it must be sent to the court with a request that it be 'issued'. This is a formal term and is used to show that the claim has been received by the court. You will receive a copy of the form with the court seal on it and a response pack.

It is your responsibility to 'serve' these documents on the other side. This means you must bring it to their attention. There are a number of ways but the most common are by sending by 1st Class post to their usual or last known residence or personally by handing them over. You must do this within 4 months of it being issued by the court.

If you receive a claim form you have 14 days to respond to it. In the pack you receive should be the defence form. If you dispute that your dog bit the other person then say so and return the form.

If you do not return the form you may find that a judgment is entered against you.

Once a defence is entered then the case will proceed to trial. Whichever side you are on you will need to ensure you gather all your evidence together and service it on the other party.

The court will set down a timetable for various things to happen. The first issue is disclosure. This requires you to conduct a reasonable search for documents in your possession. 'Documents' includes emails and text information stored on your computer; it refers to documents you want to use, documents that might help the other side or another party. You must then provide a list to the other side. This may be a vet report, a bill from your vet, a medical report, a police report, and photographs.

If there are documents they do not have, they are entitled to inspect them and have copies.

The next stage is that of witness statements. You are required to file with the court and the other party all the witness statements you will rely on. A witness statement must contain all the relevant facts. You must ensure that all your witness statements are filed – you cannot just turn up with a witness and expect them to be heard (this isn't Perry Mason).

If the other party does not accept the witness statement you will have to make arrangements for that person to be present at court. For example if the other party dispute a doctor's statement that there was a bite that could have been inflicted by a dog.

Once the court date arrives the party bringing the claim will present their evidence, if it is not agreed, by calling the witness and you will be entitled to ask them relevant questions. The other party will then have an opportunity to present their case and be asked questions.

The Judge will then make a decision on the balance of probabilities, i.e. is it more likely than not that you were bitten by the dog? If so they will go on to look at whether and how much money you should receive.

As always there will be an issue as to costs. The usual rule is that the loser pays the other party their costs. This may not be the case if the winning side unreasonably refuse to settle and received less than was offered or if there was a failure to enter into mediation.

Tips for either court

If you are involved in an incident collect as much information as you can at the time. Take photographs of any injures, of the dog who caused the issue, of the owner or person with the dog. Note down any names and addresses of people nearby. Keep copies of all vet bills.

Summary

When it goes wrong and you have to have recourse to the law there are certain procedures that you must follow to be successful. A Lawyer is often a luxury these days so hopefully this will give you some basic idea of what to expect or what you can do if it goes wrong.

IMPORTANT INFORMATION AND AIDE-MEMOIRE

IMPORTANT INFORMATION

Dog details Kennel Club name Pet name Breed Distinguishing features Health issues	
Vets Phone number Emergency number	
Microchip Company Phone Number Chip Number	
Insurance Company Policy number Telephone Number Email address	
Other Dog Legislation Officer Dog Welfare Officer Legal Advice	Andrea Pitt

AIDE-MEMOIRE

Name and address of owner Name of Dog Breed of Dog Description of dog Photo Description of owner Photo Details of incident Time and Place Witnesses What happened? Injuries to you Injuries to dog Vet opinion VET Fees	

MORE BOOKS BY LAW BRIEF PUBLISHING

'Ellis and Kevan on Credit Hire, 5th Edition' by Aidan Ellis & Tim Kevan
'RTA Allegations of Fraud in a Post-Jackson Era: The Handbook, 2nd Edition' by Andrew Mckie
'A Practical Guide to Holiday Sickness Claims' by Andrew Mckie & Ian Skeate
'RTA Personal Injury Claims: A Practical Guide Post-Jackson' by Andrew Mckie
'On Experts: CPR35 for Lawyers and Experts' by David Boyle
'An Introduction to Personal Injury Law' by David Boyle
'A Practical Guide to Running Housing Disrepair and Cavity Wall Claims' by Andrew Mckie, Ian Skeate, Simon Redfearn
'A Practical Guide to Claims Arising From Accidents Abroad and Travel Claims' by Andrew Mckie & Ian Skeate
'A Practical Guide to Cosmetic Surgery Claims' by Dr Victoria Handley
'A Practical Guide to Chronic Pain Claims' by Pankaj Madan
'A Practical Guide to Claims Arising from Fatal Accidents' by James Patience
'A Practical Approach to Clinical Negligence Post-Jackson' by Geoffrey Simpson-Scott
'A Practical Guide to Personal Injury Trusts' by Alan Robinson
'Occupiers, Highways and Defective Premises Claims: A Practical Guide Post-Jackson' by Andrew Mckie

'Employers' Liability Claims: A Practical Guide Post-Jackson' by Andrew Mckie
'A Practical Guide to Subtle Brain Injury Claims' by Pankaj Madan
'The Law of Driverless Cars: An Introduction' by Alex Glassbrook
'A Practical Guide to Costs in Personal Injury Cases' by Matthew Hoe
'A Practical Guide to Alternative Dispute Resolution in Personal Injury Claims – Getting the Most Out of ADR Post-Jackson' by Peter Causton, Nichola Evans, James Arrowsmith
'A Practical Guide to Personal Injuries in Sport' by Adam Walker & Patricia Leonard
'A Practical Guide to Marketing for Lawyers' by Catherine Bailey & Jennet Ingram
'A Practical Guide to Marketing for Lawyers' by Catherine Bailey & Jennet Ingram
'The No Nonsense Solicitors' Practice: A Guide To Running Your Firm' by Bettina Brueggemann
'Baby Steps: A Guide to Maternity Leave and Maternity Pay' by Leah Waller
'The Queen's Counsel Lawyer's Omnibus: 20 Years of Cartoons from the Times 1993-2013' by Alex Steuart Williams

These books and more are available to order online direct from the publisher at www.lawbriefpublishing.com, where you can also read free sample chapters. For any queries, contact us on 0844 587 2383 or mail@lawbriefpublishing.com.

Our books are also usually in stock at www.amazon.co.uk with free next day delivery for Prime members, and at good legal bookshops such as Hammicks and Wildy & Sons.

We are regularly launching new books in our series of practical day-to-day practitioners' guides. Visit our website and join our free newsletter to be kept informed and to receive special offers, free chapters, etc.

You can also follow us on Twitter at www.twitter.com/lawbriefpub.

Milton Keynes UK
Ingram Content Group UK Ltd.
UKHW022239280324
440266UK00007B/475